living
lag⦿m

250 + simple steps to a balanced, happier
& more sustainable life

Oliver Johansson

Not too little, not too much.
Just right. **Swedish**

living lagom

250+ simple steps to a balanced, happier & more sustainable life

Credits: imagery under license from Shutterstock

ISBN 978-1-911219-89-7

Disclaimer

BELL & MACKENZIE
PUBLISHING LIMITED

www.bellmackenzie.com

⊘ Contents

• • ◆

☉ Introduction

Lagom is equilibrium. It is a way of life that balances our wants with our needs. The ethos behind lagom is creating a happier and more sustainable lifestyle by not taking more than we need but in turn not having to make unnecessary sacrifices.

Originating from Sweden, lagom (pronounced lar-gom), dates back to the eleventh century and the age of the Vikings where communal horns filled with wine were passed around for everyone to drink their own share and not a bit more – there was just enough for everyone. In modern day Sweden it is not just a word but also now a culture that is modest, balanced and content.

It is about finding the perfect balance for you. In its simplest form lagom is 'not too much or too little....just right'.

In an increasingly uncertain financial and political world, carving a path to a simpler way of life can provide much needed stability. Rather than interpreting lagom as 'just scraping by' it is more about appropriateness and in a world of extremes and contradictions, a happier and more balanced life is more attractive. Think less in black and white terms and more on the middle ground.

Adopting a lagom lifestyle can take many forms and be applied to different areas of our everyday lives. It is not just about playing a part in protecting the planet's natural resources through energy saving practices but about balancing our work and home lives and protecting the relationships with those we love. Lagom can apply to fashion & make up, design, cooking, gardens, finances, exercise and more. It has a place in every aspect of our lives.

In the modern world we are bombarded with daily images of excess, beauty, power, perfection, money and unattainable goals. Lagom instead focuses on equally powerful messages that promote fair share, rationalisation, the collective good, acceptance and contentment.

Where translation can be lost, lagom could be negatively interpreted as 'denying oneself', 'frugality', 'just sufficient' or 'sacrifice'. The reality is quite the opposite. It is having the knowledge that life is good and we should be thankful. Yes, perhaps life could be a little better, but it's good enough. It's about acceptance and contentment. By making small changes you can make a real difference to your own life as well as the benefit of others and the planet.

To start you on the path of lagom discovery we've compiled a list of easy ways you can live lagom. Simple, life changing, life balancing suggestions and steps you can take to create a sustainable and simpler way of life that is….. just enough. Some will require a level of investment in either time or money but most will cost you nothing at all and will help you create a healthier and happier balance to your life.

⊘ Energy

Busy lives and tight budgets can make it hard to know where to start when it comes to the complex issues of personal environmental impact. Lagom isn't about trying to be too frugal or depriving yourself. It's simply about using only what you need. Using just enough. It's about reducing waste. Not reducing your enjoyment of life. It's taking the right amount and nothing more.

Try the simple ideas in the following section to make small changes towards a more balanced lagom lifestyle.

• • •

⊘ Install a programmable thermostat in your home – don't set it too high. 18-21 degrees is the optimum range for comfort in a room.

⊘ Don't let furniture block thermostats. This can give a false reading and result in your heating system having to work harder to heat the room.

⊘ Don't cover radiators or block them with furniture.

⊘ Consider comparing energy costs on a price comparison site. It's very easy to switch suppliers so check each year for the best deals.

- Use energy saving light bulbs. CFLs (Compact Fluorescent Lamps) are cost efficient alternatives for the home and could save you £5 per year for each bulb. LEDs (Light Emitting Diodes) are more efficient than CFLs and can save you more money in the long term. They are good for spotlights and dimmable lights.
- Seal window draughts with tape.
- Use door draught excluders at the bottom of doors.
- Have your home assessed by the *Energy Saving Trust.* It's free and they will give plenty of advice on energy saving measures.
- Use heavy lined curtains on your windows to retain heat and hold back cold air.
- Consider double or secondary glazing. Most heat in a room is lost through windows.

- Insulate your loft.
- Unplug and take devices off standby mode. When electrical devices are left in standby mode they are still using energy. The average household cost in electricity bills each year related to devices left on standby is £30.
- Install an insulating blanket around your water tank to retain heat.
- Insulate accessible water pipes to retain heat and reduce the risk of burst pipes in the winter.
- Don't leave the fridge door open. Each time your fridge is opened warm air from the room begins heating up the fridge so it has to work harder to keep a lower temperature.
- Use your dishwasher only when you have a full load and on an eco setting.
- Use your washing machine only with full load and on a 30 degree wash where possible.
- Only use a tumble dryer when you have to. Clean out the filter after every use to optimise drying power.

- Use timers on any lights that tend to be left on longer.
- When going on holiday turn off all electrical items that are not being used.
- When going on holiday reprogram heating, hot water, room thermostats and radiator thermostats.
- Add a reflecting panel behind radiators to reflect heat back into the room.
- Keep curtains and blinds closed at night to keep heat in. Open them in the morning to let warmth from the sun back in.
- For tiled or hardwood floors use rugs for warmth.
- If you have a wood burning stove use only dried hardwood.
- Use a microwave to reheat rather than an oven. It is far more efficient.

- Use rechargeable batteries. It's a no-brainer.
- Consider cavity wall insulation to external walls. It could save you £150 per year in heating bills.

- Consider renewable energy. There are many options available for renewable energy from solar panels to domestic wind turbines. Although they can be costly at the outset they can pay back the initially outlay in a few years.
- Draught-proof your letterbox.
- Install a chimney balloon - If you have a fireplace that is not in use you can block the chimney and reduce heat escaping by installing a simple balloon.
- Turn down the thermostat on your water tank. Does your water really need to be that hot?
- Instead of using an extractor fan open the window.
- Only buy 'A' rated appliances.
- Use motion detection lights instead of leaving lights on.
- Repair fridge door seals.
- Fill your freezer up. Less space means it won't fill

up with as much warm air each time you open it.

- Only boil as much water as you need. Don't fill the kettle up.
- Unplug your phone from the charger when the battery is full and the charger from the wall.
- Don't buy large appliances when you don't need them. For example do you really need a large American style fridge?
- Don't dry clothes on radiators – the boiler will need to work harder to heat the radiator and the room.
- Dim the brightness on your smartphone.

⊘ Recycling

Reduce the quantity of products you consume. Ok so this is quite an all-encompassing target but simplify it and try to apply to as many different areas of your life as you can. For example if something is broken can it be fixed rather than replacing? If you drink bottled water could you instead install a simple water filter to your tap and use a re-useable cup rather than repurchasing harmful plastic bottles of water that are destined for landfill.

• ● ◆

⊘   Buy recycled products wherever possible. These will be made using recycled materials and the packaging and/or marketing will verify this. A product may be marked as recyclable and while this may be a selling point, if for example there are no suitably qualified plants in the area which are capable of recycling that product then it is still likely to still end up in landfill. Similarly while the product may in fact be recyclable, the actual technology needed to recycle it may not yet exist.

⊘   Donate electronics. While most city recycling centres will separate electronic items for disposal there are non-profit organisations which will take unwanted electrical items and re-use components. For example unwanted mobile phones or computers can be reconditioned and donated to senior citizens.

- Re-use packaging. Oversized and excess packaging is a major contributor to landfill sites. If you buy a product in packaging get into the habit of thinking how that packaging could be re-used. For example returning it to the manufacturer or perhaps using it in your own home as a storage container?

- Donate to Charity. Recycling doesn't just mean your local council-run recycling centre. Charities will welcome donations of used goods you no longer need or want.

- Before disposing of anything, ask the question "can

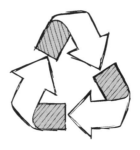

it be used by someone else?"

- Buy recycled paper.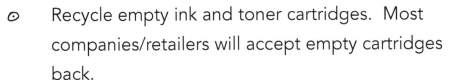
- Print on both sides of your paper.
- Recycle your paper when finished.
- Recycle empty ink and toner cartridges. Most companies/retailers will accept empty cartridges back.
- Invest in a split bin in your kitchen. Having 2 sections in your bin - one for general waste and one for recycling - makes things much easier than having to go outside or to the bottom of the stairs each time you want to add something to the recycling bin. How many times have we thrown something recyclable into general waste because we couldn't be bothered going outside?
- Use re-useable coffee cups. Contrary to what you make think, most cups from takeaway coffee outlets are not recyclable or at least recycling companies do not offer the service to recycle the cups. Take your own re-usable cup next time you buy coffee.

⊘ Water

Lagom is widely translated as 'in moderation' and when it comes to water usage nowhere should the ethos of moderation be more keenly applied. Clean, safe drinking water is scarce. Whilst 70% of the world's surface is covered by water, 97.5% of that is salt water. Only 2.5% of it is fresh water and more than half of the freshwater is frozen in ice caps and glaciers. In real terms just 1% of the total water resources on earth are available for human use. Which makes water a precious commodity. That doesn't mean you should limit your use. Not at all. Just take what you need. Nothing more.

Take a look through the following section to make sure you use only your fair share and help reduce needless waste.

• • ◆

⊘   Check taps for drips. Replacing washers on leaky taps not only stops that annoying drip but could save you up to £10 a year on your water bill.

⊘   Insulate water pipes. As well as saving energy costs by helping to retain heat in hot water pipes, insulating can also prevent burst pipes in the winter which can lose a lot of water as well as causing a lot of damage to your home.

⊘   Take a shower instead of a bath. Showers use much

less water. You could save up to 45 litres per day.

- Shower for a minute less. You will be surprised at how many litres of water you can go through in a minute.
- Go one step further when showering by turning the shower off when soaping or shampooing. The water will still be plenty hot enough when you turn it back on to rinse.
- Don't rinse dishes before putting them into the dishwasher. Dishwasher cycles don't require pre-rinsing but do scrape any waste into food recycling/ composting.
- Turn off the tap when brushing your teeth. It is recommended to brush your teeth for 2 minutes each time. A running tap can waste 6 litres a minute.

- When shaving don't have the tap running to rinse the razor. Instead put the plug in the sink and run a little water for rinsing.
- When running a tap to wait for hot or cold water to run through, use it to fill the kettle.
- Install a water butt in your garden. The average rainfall on a roof in the UK is 21,000 litres each year. Harvest this water to use in the garden.
- Ask your water provider about a smart meter. This can be a good way to monitor your water usage and reduce your bill.
- When watering your garden with a hose, use a trigger gun rather than the traditional nozzle. It has an automatic shut off and varying settings for more effective watering.
- When having a bath, put the plug in before you start running the taps and adjust the temperature as you fill.
- Let kids share the bath. When they are younger it is great fun to share the bath with some toys and uses half the water of two baths.

- No need to rinse recycling items such as tin cans and jars. The recycling process doesn't require them to be clean, only empty.
- Use the correct flush on a dual flush toilet. It may sound obvious but there is a short flush button (using less water) and a long flush button (using more water). Make sure everyone in the family knows the difference and when to use.
- Locate your stopcock. In the event of a burst pipe you can save gallons by quickly stopping the water flow and minimising damage to your home. Make sure your stopcock is easily accessible.
- Water used to rinse vegetables and salad can be also be used to water your house plants.
- If your tap water is safe (the UK has one of the most stringent water testing in the world) then avoid buying bottled water to drink.

⊘ Food Waste

The statistics for food waste in the western world are staggering. Each year we send millions of tonnes of food to landfill. This waste is often made worse by the promotion of multi-buys and other special supermarket offers which encourage us to buy more then we need. Don't get pulled into this cycle. Consider for yourself what your needs are and don't allow the supermarkets to pass on their waste to you - which is essentially what is happening when they encourage you to over-buy.

Try some of the simple ideas in the following section to cut down on food waste and do your part.

• ● ◆

⊘ Grow your own food. You don't have to be farmer with acres of land to cultivate some fantastic home grown food. If you are lucky enough to have a garden then a veg patch can yield some lovely organic produce. Alternatively, a sunny windowsill or balcony is perfect for salad and herbs – there's more on this later in the book.

⊘ Consider eating less meat. As well as the higher cost, huge areas of land are needed just to grow agricultural food for livestock or it is imported from abroad, which further depletes resources and increases pollution.

- ○ Support your local farmers market. While there can be expensive produce on sale there are some great bargains to be had for locally produced organic fruit and vegetables.

- ○ Forage for food – it's free! There is an abundance of food available for free. Just a short journey outside a city can offer everything from blackberries and gooseberries to wild garlic and mushrooms (make sure you are aware of which mushrooms to pick and which are poisonous).

- ○ Make the most of a whole chicken. It's not just the succulent breast and legs. Use left over meat for

How to Reduce Food Waste

- ○ Recycle What You Can't Eat
- ○ Eat It All or Store Leftovers for Later
- ○ Cook the Right Amount
- ○ Store Correctly
- ○ Buy What You Need
- ○ Plan Ahead

sandwiches, the brown meat is great in a curry and the carcass makes a fantastic stock.

- Save a portion for lunch. When cooking an evening meal, the chances are you will have made too much. Divide a portion and store for lunch the next day.

- Think of leftovers as ingredients. Too much rice can make burritos, too much pasta makes a great cold pasta salad and extra vegetables can make a great pasta sauce.

- Use stale bread. The end of a loaf that's just past its best is great for making breadcrumbs in a food processor or bake in the oven to dip into olive oil and balsamic vinegar.

- Store and freeze. Invest in food storage containers and prep your meals for the week.

- Be inventive with the contents of your fridge. Once a week make a point of taking out all the leftovers and half opened jars in your fridge. Be creative and see what you can concoct into an evening meal.

- If you don't have the option of composting, keep

vegetable scraps in the freezer to use for stock. Onions, herbs, carrots, greens, corn etc can all be boiled up with a bay leaf and some peppercorns to make a great veggie stock.

- Freeze large portions. Buying large cuts of meat for example, can save money in the long run but if you are unlikely to use it straight away, divide and freeze for another day. Similarly a loaf of bread will go past its best after a few days. If you live on your own and are unlikely to use a whole loaf, split half of it and freeze.

- Eat a little less. More often than not we all eat too much. Think about your portion sizes and only eat what satisfies you. You will soon get into the habit of making 'just right' quantities.

- When cooking, use the correct ring on your stove to

match the size of your saucepan. Don't put a small pan on a large ring.

- Consider stack cooking. Specially designed cookware allows you to cook and warm multiple foods on a single burner.
- Steam. Steaming is very healthy way to cook. An electric steamer will use less energy than gas and allows you to layer food so you can cook multiple dishes at once.
- If you are considering a new cooker think about an induction option. Induction hobs work by transferring energy through the base of the pan and only work when the pan is sitting on the hob. This saves wasted energy and is a very responsive and controllable way to cook.
- Prepare a shopping list. It might sound obvious but if you take the time to make a good shopping list and plan your meals you are less likely to impulse-buy unnecessary items.
- Shop by yourself. If you take your kids to the supermarket there will be all kinds of unplanned purchases.

- Don't shop when you are hungry. You are more likely to make poor food choices.
- Many of the larger supermarkets now have sections with reduced priced items. These are products that are close to their sell-by or use-by date. They are not inferior and there is nothing wrong with them. Make the most of these items - many of them can be frozen as soon as you get home.
- Cook one-pot meals such as casseroles and stews. They are easy to prepare, make use of leftovers and require less washing up. They can also freeze well for another day.
- Buy produce in season. Fruit and vegetables that are in season are one of the best ways to get the most of their nutrition. Also when they are in abundance in season they are likely to be cheaper

than out of season produce that is imported and flown in from thousands of miles away.

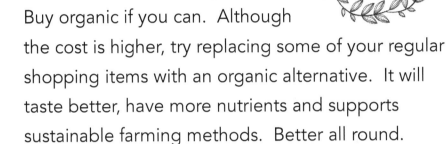

- Buy organic if you can. Although the cost is higher, try replacing some of your regular shopping items with an organic alternative. It will taste better, have more nutrients and supports sustainable farming methods. Better all round.

⊙ Grow Your Own

Nothing epitomises the spirit of lagom more than growing your own food. Both gratifying and liberating, growing fruit and vegetables puts you in tune with the rhythm of nature and provides a seasonal structure you can live by.

What's more, by learning to grow your own food you will develop skills which you can pass on, teaching others how to grow their own produce too..

Whether you have access to a garden, a balcony, a deck, a roof, a patch of ground or no more than a windowsill you can still get involved and learn to grow your own food on the space you have.

• ● ◆

Things to consider………

⊙   **Planning** - Determine which crops you can grow in your location. Amongst other things you'll need to take account of available space, climate, soil and rainfall.

⊙   **Seasons** – figure out how the seasons work and when is the right time of year to start your growing journey. Most will be for sowing in spring/summer but some will have winter options too.

Get to know your crops and figure out how they'll fit into your lifestyle:

- ⊘ **Vegetables** are a great provider of nutrients, minerals and vitamins. They can be a good source of protein & complex carbohydrates as well as minerals.
- ⊘ **Herbs & salads** offer some of the easiest things to grow and give you fast fresh options for meals and cooking.
- ⊘ **Fruit** not only offers many of the nutrients you'll find in vegetables they can also boast a broad variety of tastes to enjoy as well as lending themselves to preserving and drying.

Work out the cost. There is no point spending a fortune to grow a little. Start off small. You'll only need to spend pennies that way.

Easy to grow......

○ **Salad leaves** come in many shapes and sizes and offer a fantastic range of textures and flavours. Some grow so quickly you could be cutting fresh leaves to eat in just 3 weeks time.

○ **Spring onions and radishes** are both very quick-growing vegetables. They can be grown in the ground or in pots and containers.

○ **Potatoes** are a fun and easy crop to grow. Originating from 'seed potatoes' they can be grown in the ground, in containers or in potato bags – suitable for even the smallest spaces. With plenty of varieties you'll be able to find a potato that suits both your space and eating needs.

○ **Peas** are usually sweet and trouble free! Start them in the spring and enjoy fresh pods in the summer. They need a little support to grow tall but they generally look after themselves.

○ **Mint, Basil, Chives & Coriander.** These vigorous and fast growing herbs, and others, are ideal for growing in pots on windowsills with plenty of sunlight. Having fresh grown herbs to hand will alter your cooking and eating habits forever.

- **Cucumbers** like sunlight and warm temperatures as well as support for climbing. The bush variety is ideal for growing in containers if you are short of space.

- **Broad beans** develop into really robust plants that will give you a great deal of pleasure to see growing. What's more they have beautiful flowers that attract bees to give your garden that lovely buzzing feeling.

- **Runner Beans.** Similar to broad beans this crop doesn't take much looking after. They are a climbing plant and need some height so if you are short of space try a dwarf runner bean.

- **Onions & Garlic.** Both of these versatile crops are

virtually maintenance free. Plant the onion bulbs and garlic cloves in spring (or autumn) in well-drained beds or containers. Lift  them when they are ready and leave them to dry out in the sun.

- ○ **Tomatoes.** Grow from seed or seedlings. Tomatoes need lots of sunlight and a little heat. They are ideal for growing in compost bags and containers. Some varieties are even suited to hanging baskets.

- ○ **Beetroot.** For an easy to grow root vegetable, try beetroot. Sow seeds March to July and enjoy the colourful bulbs just 8-12 weeks later.

- ○ **Courgettes** are one of the most satisfying vegetables to grow with a bountiful crop bursting from beautiful flowers. You need quite a bit of space for the unwieldy plants that grow quickly and vigorously. Look after your courgette plants well and you'll virtually see them grow minute by minute.

- ○ **Carrots.** Easy to grow in the ground, carrots are also good for containers although they might not grow quite so big. They like the sun but can also survive in a partially shaded spot too.

- ◎ **Strawberries** are so versatile that they can be grown in containers, hanging baskets and window boxes. Try a variety that will extend the summer harvest period.
- ◎ **Blueberries** are an ideal fruit for growing in containers if you are short of space. They are a year-round joy offering scented flowers in spring, beautiful leaves in autumn and sweet berries in the summer.
- ◎ **Figs** offer something a little different and can be easy to cultivate if you have a hot, sunny south/west-facing wall. They may take quite a while to grow but their delicious Mediterranean fruit is worth the wait!
- ◎ **Apples**. If you have space, plant a tree. Nothing

beats an established apple tree and there are a multitude of varieties to suit every size of garden.

○ **Blackberries** are perfect for any scrappy bit of garden you might have spare as they'll pretty much grow in any rough corner you can find. Train the stems around wires to make them easier to pick or try a thorn-less variety.

⊘ Home Styling

Adopting lagom in your home isn't always about spending a lot of money or even making big changes but rather about making improvements to the small or everyday things which can make a big difference.

Furthermore, making small changes to your everyday life while minimising environmental impact is striving towards a lagom lifestyle.

• • ◆

⊘ Buy bamboo products. Bamboo can be harvested without the use of pesticides, it regenerates very quickly and is strong. Bamboo can be used in a multitude of ways from beautiful flooring, blinds, baskets and pots to clothing and bed linen.

⊘ Use acacia wood. Acacia is an ancient wood from trees and shrubs that are found in warm climates. It is known for its almost indestructible nature which makes it very durable and long lasting – perfect for outdoors. If it's time to replace some garden furniture consider acacia wood to make it last.

⊘ Green up your living space. Bringing the outside in

creates a sense of balance in the home and reminds us of the joy of nature. Indoor plants and potted herbs are perfect.

- Choose pale colours when decorating. The Swedes are masters of beautiful, minimalistic design and part of this is created by keeping tones neutral.

- Choose layers of monochrome. Pale doesn't need to mean just plain white. Tones of white, creams and greys are better than bold colours.

- Create warmth in your home with texture and materials rather than bold wall patterns or paint. In a neutrally decorated room add warmth with pastel throws and textured cushions.

- Bare your floors. If you are lucky enough to have original wood flooring, consider losing your carpet and embracing the warmth of a natural wood floor.

You can still use rugs for texture and comfort under foot.

- Go vintage shopping. Rather than buy new, buy old. There are amazing vintage furniture or antique shops which will have alwys have something to compliment your current living space, perhaps contrasting modern clean lines with more traditional accessories.
- Swap furniture. Before heading out to buy new items, try swapping some furniture from one room to another to breathe new life and balance into it. For example, moving the living room armchair that's seen better days into the bedroom with a casual throw can change the dynamic, immediately providing a corner for sanctuary where normally you wouldn't spend much time. The space left in the living room might actually be welcome in what may have been an overcrowded space?
- Work with what you have. Your home may have some beautiful features that are worth exposing. Could exposing the old wooden beams in your kitchen ceiling contrast beautifully with your

modern units and appliances? Is there a stone hearth in your living room that has been covered over by carpet? Exposing it could bring a feature to your room you didn't know you had – and costs you nothing.

- Live with less. Do you really need everything in your room? Does every item add something to the room? Could it be used elsewhere, recycled or up-cycled?

- Buying new? If you are buying something new, try swapping it out for something old. Could that old item be used elsewhere in the home?

Use wasted space.

- Make use of space under the stairs by converting into bespoke shelves and drawers.

- Consider bespoke cupboards. Most homes

have awkward spaces or nooks and crannies that with a little professional expertise could be utilised for space. Small spaces  or unconventional layouts could provide functional storage space.

- Use recessed space for storage. Perhaps you have a chimney running through your room creating a recess either side. These could be utilised for storage or shelving.
- Maximise wall space. Hallways and porches are often under utilised in terms of wall space. With some clever thinking, walls can be transformed for hanging, storing and displaying to make the most of your space in a clutter free way. Try searching on *www.houzz.co.uk* for inspiration.
- Add chairs to hallways. Hallways are rarely used other than as a connection between rooms. Try adding some seating to your hallway. If it's long and narrow perhaps an old church pew or narrow bench with some fitted cushions. You will be surprised how much use it will get either while

you're waiting for others to get ready before leaving the house or simply as a new place to sit and read.

- Utilise space under benches. By adding baskets under benches in porches or hallways you make use of the additional space for shoes.

De-clutter

- Reduce furniture. Remember that lagom is "not too much, not too little…just right". Keep your room minimal but still functional and inviting.
- Get rid of magazines more than one month old. Your home should not resemble a doctor's waiting room.
- Keep your coffee tables mostly clear. Aim for 75% clear.
- Find a home for your remote controls. If you have

more than one then a small wicker basket will keep them tidy and stop them getting lost.

- Purge your book collection. Bulging bookshelves can be remedied by keeping only the most important books. You don't have to keep every book you've read – only the ones that have impacted your life.
- Have a corner of the room with a lightweight storage box for kid's toys (Ikea is perfect for these). Don't make it too big – smaller boxes will encourage you not to throw too many toys in it.
- Keep your kitchen worktops clear. They are easier to clean and bring that minimalistic Scandi feel.
- Purge your wardrobe. If you haven't worn an item in 3 months, consider taking it to a charity shop. If it's a seasonal item, fold and place in a vacuum bag or storage box in a corner of your wardrobe for next season.

⊘ Work/Life Balance

Perhaps one of the most important aspects of lagom is that of work/life balance. In the UK and the western world in general, we are working more and more as we struggle to balance out the need to work with our need for personal happiness and that of our family. Technology has compounded this problem, making us accessible 24 hours a day.

In Sweden, normal working hours are 40hrs per week from 8.30/9.00am to 5.00pm although some companies are also moving to a six-hour working day (30hour week) as a means of increasing productivity and to make people happier. It is worth noting that most Swedish employees go home at 5pm to take care of their families. More so than in any other country, employees in Sweden believe that overtime is not valued or necessary. Furthermore additional hours can also be viewed as poor planning or time management. Remember that lagom is about balance.

● ● ◆

⊘   Have set working hours and stick to them.

Although it may not always be possible to contain

your working week to 40 hours, you can still allocate

time to work and time to rest. So for example

commit to not getting into the office before 9am

each day and to leaving by 6.30pm no matter how busy you are.

- Set aside a full hour during the day to leave your place of work, have some lunch and get some fresh air. Although you may argue you don't have the time, the break from the office will recharge your mind and body making you more productive when you return.

- Delegate. Whether it is at work or at home there may be others who can take some of your workload/chores and do them just as well (maybe better). Focus on what you are good at and what must be done that day.

- Make the best of your most productive time. For example are you a morning person or maybe you just can't really get going until midday? Prioritise

your most demanding tasks according to when you are most alert.

- Make a 'to do' list. Before the end of each day list the key things you need to achieve the following day. This will put your mind at ease knowing what the focus for the following day is going to be.

- Remember that you work to live, not live to work. It's become a cliché but worth remembering now and again.

- Make a comfortable workspace. If you can, take some measures that will make your working day more comfortable. For example sitting on an ergonomic chair, using a stand for your laptop to bring it to eye level or perhaps a standing station so your posture is better whilst working.

- Have a workspace just for work. If you work from home try to choose a space or room in your home that is used just for work so you can close the door at the end of each day. Although many of us work from the kitchen table, the tendency is to leave our laptops open all day and night constantly dipping in and out. If you can't have a separate space, have a cupboard where you place your laptop and files at the end of each day out of sight.

- Learn to say 'no'. You don't have to agree to do everything you are asked.

- Consider employing a cleaner at home if you can afford it. Free up a couple of hours normally spent cleaning each week and replace that time with an outdoor activity with the family.

- Shop online for groceries. The first time you do this will be time consuming but after that you can easily do a weekly shop in 15 minutes – much easier and less stressful than a trip to the supermarket and gives you back at least one hour of your time each week.

#FREEDOM

- Switch off your phone before you enter the house at the end of your working day. If you can, put it away in a drawer or in your jacket pocket so you are not tempted to switch it on each time you pass it.

- Don't feel the need to reply to emails immediately. Make it clear to colleagues that you will reply to them in a reasonable period of time. If the email is not urgent, an urgent response is not required.

- Get into the habit of not checking your emails when you are not at work. Remember that most of the time whoever is sending the email will not expect you to read it until the next day.

- Make plans for a holiday and give yourself time off every 3 months.

- Stretch. Stop what your are doing at least twice a day, stretch your arms and legs, roll your shoulders forwards and backwards and rotate your neck and head. Breathe.

- Meet a friend or colleague for coffee. If you work for yourself it can often be lonely. Take time to arrange to get out of your workplace even if it's just for 15 minutes.
- Don't take your phone to bed. The bright light from the screen stimulates and makes it difficult to wind down and sleep.
- Pace yourself. There are times and situations when we need to accelerate our pace to meet a deadline. Understand when a quicker pace is required and when it is not. Living a more balanced working life will lead to better health, productivity and happiness.
- Exercise. It is proven that exercise helps us achieve a healthy body which in turn will make our bodies function better. Prioritise exercise each week as

much as you do for your work tasks.

○ Meet halfway. If you need to meet clients suggest a hallway point. You don't always have to travel the other side of town (or the country) to meet them. Even better, can a Skype video call suffice and save you even more of your valuable time?

○ Consider others. If you have a partner or family at home consider their time. They may or may not have also been working or looking after children but at the end of the day they will be looking forward to unwinding and spending time with you. Try to plan and arrange your day so that time with your loved ones after working hours is special.

○ Plan a mid week social event. Arranging to catch up with friends, or taking out your partner for dinner helps break up the week. It's something to look forward to and a way to blow off steam should you have a particularly stressful day.

○ Embrace flexible hours. Perhaps one day of the week your child needs picking up from school. Talk to your superior about working from home that afternoon each week to allow you to fulfil your family responsibilities. The chances are you will still achieve everything you would have done in the office, if not more.

○ Don't read emails on the commute. If you travel to work on public transport, instead of spending that time looking through your emails (or social media), use the time to read a book. You will find you look forward to the commute more if you are engrossed in a good book.

○ Sleep. Aim for 7-8 hours per night. Set a time for bed to achieve the optimum sleep time and stick to it. Don't take your phone to bed!

⊘ Garden Styling

Creating a beautiful Scandinavian inspired garden like any landscaping project requires a fair amount of planning but if you want to take inspiration from the Swedes it isn't necessary to completely rework your garden. Remember that lagom is all about moderation – 'not too little, not too much. Just right.' With this in mind there are many small alterations you can make to your garden which can help you create a balanced and soothing outdoor space.

• • ◆

⊘   To achieve a lagom ambiance to your outdoor space think clean and simple lines, pale colours and natural wood. Your garden should be natural and minimalist and easy to maintain.

⊘   De-clutter your garden. Have a really good tidy up; store any tools and children's toys away in a shed if you have one, round the side of your house or if possible to a less imposing place in the garden.

⊘   Add splashes of colour but don't be too bold. Choose a favourite plant pot and paint in a muted pastel colour for example.

⊘   Mix and match your planters. They don't all have to

be the same design but try to keep in mind simple and clean looking. The choice of plants you put in them is more important.

- ○ Choose alpine inspired flowers and planters such as Wolf Bane and Alpine Milk Vetch or Tiger Lilly. Blues, pale pinks and lilacs are all good colours to aim for when browsing your local garden centre.

- ○ Plant evergreen shrubs to keep your garden green all year round. Some good hardy examples are Daphne which flowers in winter and spring, Lavender for its beautiful fragrance and lilac flowers and Aucuba which is great in shaded areas of a garden.

- ○ Plant fruit bushes – there is nothing more satisfying than fruit picking especially when it's from your own garden – try blackberry or gooseberry.

- Find a sheltered but sunny corner of the garden for growing your own herbs. They emit beautiful fragrances and are perfect for  the kitchen. Grow whatever you use most in the kitchen.

- Choose natural wood garden furniture. This can be expensive so only consider once your current furniture needs replacing (or up-cycling). Natural wood furniture gives the feeling of being close to nature and ideally it should be from a sustainable source. Acacia wood is a good choice because it is very durable and should last for years.

- Add some candles to your garden. These add warmth and ambiance and balance your garden beautifully on a summer's evening.

- Consider a fire pit or chiminea. In the UK the summer evenings can be cool so having the heat from a wood-burning fire from a sustainable wood source can extend your time outdoors.

- Build a canopy. If your garden space allows for it, a canopy can be a welcome addition to any garden.

It provides shelter and shade and a natural place for table and chairs. A traditional style pergola would work - if you have a sunny position grow wisteria over it for a lovely leafy feature.

- If your garden feels overly concrete, don't be tempted to rush out and replace all your patio slabs. By introducing cottage style plants throughout you will be able to balance and soften the more structural and hard elements of your space.
- Think tall and short. Get the balance right by choosing some tall plants as well as shorter ones. Foxglove and African Queen are good examples.
- Don't over-think your garden. Remember it's not a show home – it's a place for you to relax, have fun and entertain now and again. It should be a place

Purple foxglove

to give you an uncluttered sense of wellbeing.

○ See *Grow Your Own Section* for more ideas.

⊘ Finances

Getting your finances in order is key to following a lagom lifestyle as it gives you a feeling of stability and peace when you are not overspending and stressing out over money.

Some people may just need a system for keeping track of their spending whilst others may be in debt and need strategies to help them find a way out.

• ● ◆

Tips For Keeping Your Finances Stable:

⊘ Savings account: Save money by setting up a standing order which goes straight out of your bank into a savings account each week or month. Everyone needs an emergency fund for those unforeseen things that always come up.

⊘ Make better choices: Try to control your impulse spending. Before you buy something consider if you really need it to make you happy.

⊘ Track your spending: Set up a spread sheet and work out your outgoings and income. Having everything in front of you on one document will help make your finances clear.

⊘ Pay bills on time: Set up standing orders and direct debits for your bills. Often they may be discounted if you pay by this method and it means you don't pick up penalties or fees.

Debt

⊘ If you don't have debt DON'T START now. Debt equals unhappiness and slavery.

⊘ If you do have debt START GETTING OUT OF IT. Look at the tips in next section.

Tips To Help You Get Out Of Debt

⊘ Admit there is a problem: Until you do that you can't make a start with anything. The first step is admitting you have a problem. Stop ignoring it and once you have admitted it, give yourself a specific

time each week to review your
finances and to deal with any
issues.

- Don't make it any worse: It's time
to stop. Stop throwing good money after bad. Stop
digging the hole you are in even deeper.
- For one whole month do not make any purchases at
all unless it is a 'survival' purchase. That means you
don't buy it unless you need it to stay alive.
- Cutting back: This is getting to the meat of
everyday living. Stop buying brands. You don't
need them. Shop's own brands are often just as
good.
- If you eat out a lot or buy lunch at work - Stop.
Make food at home and eat there or take it out with
you.
- Rainy days fund: Everyone needs an emergency
fund. Unexpected things come up and these are
often the things that can throw a debt plan out of
the window. So make a start on an emergency fund
- once you've worked out how much money you
save by cutting back each month start diverting this

to your 'rainy day' fund.

- Take stock: It's time to set up a simple spread sheet. In one column, list all of your debts, credit cards, loans, etc.

  In another column, put the amounts you owe for each debt.

  In the third column, put the minimum monthly payment you can make on each of these debts. This way you'll be able to figure this your total debt owed and how much you have to pay, at a mini mum, towards the debt each month. Making min imum monthly payment will at least stop your debt increasing.

- Make a budget: Now you know the extent of your debt, figure out your monthly living budget. List your monthly outgoings (bills, food, petrol etc).

Plus write down the minimum monthly debt payment that you have already worked out from the last point. Now, list your income  sources so you know what you've got to work with.

⊘ Pay bills on time: Don't let further debts build up with late fees and charges. If you want to get out of debt you need to pay your bills.

Quick Tips:

⊘ Praise: Make sure you praise yourself for making the right choices.

⊘ Change: Focus on changing your behaviour and attitude.

⊘ Be realistic: If you have been in debt for years it's not realistic to think you are going to get out of debt overnight. It's a slow process. Stick with it.

⊘ Is it necessary? Take a hard look at what's truly necessary, and be willing to make compromises. You'll be amazed at how much of a difference a few changes can make.

⊘ Peer pressure: Consider how much of what you buy

is dictated by what people around you are doing. Think about what you need for your life. Not what everyone else has got.

○ Think positive: Every time you make a payment and don't increase your debt you are moving one step closer to freedom. Keep that goal in your mind.

○ Try something new: See what's going on in your local community for free. Try being a tourist in your own town, you'll find there is lots to do all around if you seek it out.

⊘ Community/Giving Back

Living lagom means having a social conscience. An everyday awareness that the greater good represents a key difference. Swedish streets are litter-free not because of the fear of fines but because Swedes understand that dropping litter would make the street less enjoyable for other people. This idea of community and giving back is at the heart of the spirit of lagom. Here's how you can get involved....

• • ◆

10 in 30 – Ten ways you can make a positive impact on your local community in less than thirty minutes.

⊘ Pick up litter: Take a bag out with you whenever you walk around your local area to collect any litter. You'll get some exercise and improve the local environment.

⊘ Shop local: Whenever you can, try shopping at locally owned businesses. You are supporting your local community, and if you walk there rather than driving to out-of-town retail parks you'll be making a positive impact.

⊘ Positive Attitude: Seek out positive things in your

community and share these with other people.
If you hear about a new club or initiative try and
support it and use social networks to spread the
word.

O Support local events: Attend a local event or
activity. Lots of towns and cities have activities with
free admission. Many of these are sponsored events
so if you support them they are more likely to run
again and increase the vibrancy in your community.

O Connect with local government: Get in touch with
you local elected representative. Let them know
they are appreciated and perhaps share a concern
you may have about the local community. People
work harder when they know they are appreciated.

O Outside space: If you have a drive, path, garden or
gate, make your immediate environment feel like a

welcoming area by growing herbs and leaving them for people to help themselves. Try writing some inspiring words on a chalkboard  at your gate to spread positive vibes. You could even set up an honesty box to sell things – it makes people feel they are living in a trustworthy environment that in turn spreads positivity.

- Get to know your neighbours: Try including a neighbour in a family meal. Or if they can't come over maybe take a meal over to an elderly or lonely person.
- Schools: If you have the time, think about helping out at a local school. Schools are often looking for local helpers to enable them to run lunchtime or afterschool clubs.
- Collecting: Many organisations collect items, such as food, clothes, toys etc. for fundraising. See if you have anything around your house which might be useful.
- Go on-line: There are now many local social networks which can help people connect. This can

range from asking for loans of garden equipment to having someone look after your dog for the day. It's a great way to up-cycle and to give neighbourly support. Try sites like *www.nextdoor.co.uk* or *www.streetlife.com*

10 More Ways To Give Back:

- Give blood: Giving blood really is like sharing a part of yourself and you never know when you may need this vital resource yourself.
- Mentoring: Consider acting as a mentor to a young person. You'll not only help them through a formative time in their life but you'll also likely learn something new about yourself.
- Senior Citizens: Consider becoming a companion or visitor for an elderly person. This may just mean

BLOOD DONATION

picking up a local paper for them each day or a weekly visit. There are lots of charities that can help connect you with people in need.

- Share your skills: Think about the skills you have to offer and consider if you could use them anywhere to benefit your local community and beyond.

- Raise & run: Consider setting yourself a task to complete a 5k, 10k or half marathon. Collect sponsorship for this and donate it to a charity close to your heart, or run to raise awareness for a particular cause you feel strongly about. Not only will you do the cause good you'll do yourself good as you improve your health and fitness.

- Be an organ donor: Opt into the organ donation program. Doing so could save so many other people's lives.

- Shop clever: Try to consider where you buy some of your consumer goods. Many retailers (big and small) support charities and causes. For example the shoe manufacturer *Toms* operates a 'one for one' scheme: every time you buy a pair of shoes they donate a pair to a child in need - so far over 60 million pairs of shoes have been given away in this manner.

- Animal lover?: Local animal shelters are often looking for extra help. While it might often be the unglamorous tasks which you will be undertaking, you'll likely also get to spend some quality time with some needy animals who will appreciate your attention.
- Share your pet: If you've got your own pet think about how it makes you smile and ask yourself if it could help make someone else smile too! Perhaps bringing your pet to a local senior centre, veteran's club or hospital to bring some joy to the residents.
- Guerrilla gardening: Consider planting a tree or flowers in a neglected space in your local area.

DONATE

It could transform an unloved
waste area into a place of beauty
overnight.

10 Small Random Acts Of Kindness

- ⊘ Practicing random kindness while expecting nothing
  in return is life affirming and costs you nothing at
  all.
- ⊘ Praise someone at work for a job well done when
  the occasion arises.
- ⊘ Send someone you know who is going through a
  difficult time a card or message to let them know
  that you care and are thinking of him or her.
- ⊘ Next time someone is rude or inconsiderate
  to you, instead of getting defensive try to be
  compassionate for that person's situation. Maybe
  they are going through a tough time and need a bit
  of understanding?
- ⊘ Express your gratitude to someone who has made a
  difference in your life.
- ⊘ Thank a service provider in your community such as

a postman, police officer or refuse worker for their hard work.

- Talk to a person at a party or gathering who is struggling with socialising.

- Cheer up a loved one by giving them an unexpected gift. You don't need to spend a lot; it's the thought that counts.

- Hide notes of encouragement in your partner or child's coat pocket.

- Call someone who you haven't talked to in a while and let them know that you've been thinking about them.

- Let someone who only has a few items in their basket go ahead of you at the checkout in the supermarket.

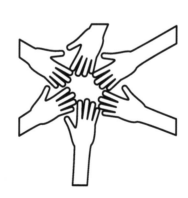

⊘ Mindfulness

A simple way to mindfulness, thankfulness & contentment.
Living lagom can often mean changing just a few habits in
order to see a big difference. That includes changing the
way we interact with others and the way we view the world
around us.
If you are living in the moment, if you are mindful of
the present… you are living lagom. Improving overall
wellbeing is just as important as any other aspect of your
life when it comes to feeling in control and getting the
balance right.

● ● ◆

Being mindful is about bringing attention to the present.

⊘ Practice it as much as you can.

⊘ Be aware.

⊘ Be alive.

⊘ Be in the moment.

⊘ Be aware of your body throughout the day. Now

and again take a minute to do any of the following:

Face – Think about the muscles in your face.

Actively relax your jaw, your eye, forehead etc.

Neck & shoulders – Relax your shoulders. Move

them down away from your ears. Roll your head around and loosen your neck.

Posture –Sraighten up your spine when you are standing, sitting or walking. Breathe deeply and walk tall.

In your everyday life, when you interact with the world try the following:

- ⊘ Eye contact - Focus on making eye contact with others, on really seeing them.
- ⊘ Listening - Truly listen to what others are saying. Don't just think about when it's your turn to speak.
- ⊘ Practice gratitude - Think daily about the things you are grateful for and vocalise them.
- ⊘ Breathing – Every now and again stop what you are doing. Sit or stand up straight and take three

deep breaths. Feel the sensation
of your breath and its journey
through your body.

Being mindful doesn't have to be practiced in a
controlled meditative state or environment. You can
practice mindfulness and be in the moment even when
you are doing something seemingly mindless.

Try paying attention to the sight and sounds around you
and how your body feels when you are doing any of the
following:

- Brushing teeth
- Taking a shower
- Drinking a coffee
- Eating a meal
- Walking to work

☉ Yoga

Yoga is a mind and body practice dating back centuries. Known for its benefits in helping build strength, balance and flexibility, it is equally significant for mindfulness and calm. With carefully selected poses that focus on breathing and relaxation, yoga can be performed almost anywhere.

• • ◆

Relaxation Routine. This gentle routine is ideal for preparing for bed, winding down in the evening or if you wish to meditate/rest throughout the day. You will need to have a mat and some pillows to hand and it should take no more than 30 minutes.

- Pose 1: Cow
- Pose 2: Cat
- Pose 3: Bridge Pose
- Pose 4: Legs Up The Wall
- Pose 5: Seated Forward Bend
- Pose 6: Wide Leg Forward Bend
- Pose 7: Cobra
- Pose 8: Left Nostril Breathing

⊙ Cow

Come onto your hands and knees with hips placed over the knees. Shoulders positioned over the wrists. Your knees and hands should be shoulder distance apart, and the spine neutral. On exhalation gently lift your tail bone up to the sky, let your belly drop toward the mat and look up. Hold for a few moments before going into the next pose.

⊙ Cat

On a breath exhalation, lengthen your tail bone to the ground, draw the belly up to the spine and round the upper back like a cat. Concentrate on pressing your hands into the mat to open the shoulder blades. Let the head drop. Gently and slowly move through ten rounds of Cat/Cow, then return to a neutral spine.

⊘ Bridge Pose

On your mat lie down with feet flat on the floor hip-width apart. Place your hands beside you with palms facing down. Engage your thighs and core and on exhalation lift your body up so that your back is flat and your knees are at a 45 degree angle whilst your arms remain flat on the floor. Settle into the pose and hold it for 2-3 minutes if you can.

⊘ Legs Up The Wall

Position yourself on your mat side-on close up to wall. Roll onto your back with your legs up in the air. Twist yourself around 90 degrees so that your legs rest straight up against the wall. Shuffle your bottom up tight against the wall if you need to. Keep your arms straight by your side with the palms flat down. Remain in this pose for 5 minutes breathing deeply and slowly, concentrating on nothing other than movement and feeling of your breath.

⊘ Seated Forward Bend

Sit on the mat with your legs straight out in front of you. Place pillow(s) on your thighs against your stomach (you may need to experiment with the height of the support). Put your arms above your head then reach forward as you bend your body onto the pillow and rest the side of your head onto the pillow support. Allow your arms to rest by your side and remain in this position for 5 minutes.

⊘ Cat

This is a variation on the last pose. This time move your legs apart whilst you are in an upright sitting position. Place your cushion(s) onto the floor between your legs. Put your arms above your head then reach forward as you bend your body onto the pillow and rest the side of your head onto the pillow support – use the opposite side of your head from the last pose. Allow your arms to rest by your side and remain in this position for 5 minutes. If this feels uncomfortable it can be helpful to sit on a block or cushion to lift your pelvis or/and you may wish to bend your knees a little.

⊙ Cobra

Lie face-down on mat. With elbows bent place palms a little away from each side of your body in line with the breastbone. Come onto fingertips and point elbows toward sky and out to sides Press pelvis, toes, and fingertips into floor. On exhalation straighten the arms enough to lift the chest off the mat. Keep the spine long and tip the head back. Hold for 8 full deep breaths before relaxing back onto the mat.

⊙ Left Nostril Breathing

Sit in a comfortable cross- legged position. Keep your back straight with your shoulders low down away from your ears. Try to imagine a piece of string being pulled from above lifting the crown of your head up towards the sky. Cover your right nostril with your thumb or finger and begin breathing in and out through your left nostril. Breathe like this for at least 2 minutes. This may seem strange but breathing through the left nostril has a calming effect on the nervous system and aids mediation and restful sleep.

⊙ You may also enjoy...

Hygge: Comfort & Food For The Soul

A cosy collection of comfort food, drinks & lifestyle
recipes for you, your friends & family to enjoy

BELL & MACKENZIE
PUBLISHING LIMITED
www.bellmackenzie.com

21689913R00051

Printed in Great Britain
by Amazon